The Everyday Cooking Collection

SEAFOOD
DELIGHTS

Licensed and produced by:

DIRECT SOURCE
SPECIAL PRODUCTS INC.

©℗1999 DIRECT SOURCE SPECIAL PRODUCTS INC.
Canada: P.O. Box 361,
Victoria Station, Westmount,
Quebec, Canada
H3Z 2V8
U.S.: P.O. Box 2189,
609 New York Road, Plattsburgh,
New York, 12903

Recipes and photos courtesy of:
Les Éditions Multi-Concept Inc.

Printed in Canada

ISBN# 1-896306-50-0

The Everyday Cooking Collection

FISH AND POTATO SOUP

4 SERVINGS

Preparation Time: 20 minutes

Cooking Time: 35 minutes

1 tbsp	(15 ml) corn oil
1/2 cup	(125 ml) chopped onion
1/2 cup	(125 ml) sliced leeks
1/2 cup	(125 ml) cubed carrots
1/2 cup	(125 ml) sliced celery
1 tsp	(5 ml) minced garlic
1 cup	(250 ml) dry white wine (optional)
2 cups	(500 ml) fish stock, skimmed of fat
1 1/2 cups	(375 ml) diced potatoes
2	tomatoes, peeled, seeded and diced
1	frond of fennel
1	bay leaf
	salt and pepper, to taste
4 oz	(125 g) haddock fillets
8	mussels, washed, cleaned and shelled
1 cup	(250 ml) milk
2 tbsp	(25 ml) chopped, fresh basil
1	slice of bread, toasted and quartered

In a large pot, heat the oil and lightly sauté the onion, leeks, carrots, celery and garlic.

Add the white wine, fish stock, potatoes, tomatoes, fennel and bay leaf. Season and let simmer for 20 minutes.

Cut the haddock fillets into bite sized pieces; add to the soup, along with the mussels. Let simmer for 10 minutes over low heat. Add the milk and keep warm. When ready to serve, garnish with basil and toasted bread.

MAPLE SEAFOOD SOUP

4 TO 6 SERVINGS
Preparation Time: 20 minutes
Cooking Time: 35 minutes

2 tbsp	(25 ml)	olive oil
1/3 cup	(75 ml)	chopped onions
3/4 cup	(175 ml)	leeks, julienned
1/3 cup	(75 ml)	carrots, julienned
1/2 cup	(125 ml)	celery, julienned
1 tsp	(5 ml)	minced garlic
28 oz	(796 ml)	crushed, peeled tomatoes
1/4 cup	(50 ml)	chopped, fresh basil or 1 tsp (5 ml) dried basil
1 tbsp	(15 ml)	chopped, fresh oregano or 1/2 tsp (2 ml) dried oregano
1		bay leaf, stalk of thyme, and sprig of parsley
3 cups	(750 ml)	fish or chicken stock, skimmed of fat
1/4 cup	(50 ml)	Chicoutai liqueur
2 tbsp	(25 ml)	maple syrup
24		mussels, cleaned and debearded
8		jumbo shrimp, shelled and deveined
12		scallops
6 oz	(180 g)	salmon fillets, cut into cubes
5 oz	(142 g)	clams, drained
		salt and pepper, to taste
		fresh parsley, chopped

In a pot, heat the oil and lightly sauté the onion, leeks, carrots and celery. Add the garlic, tomatoes, basil, oregano, bay leaf, thyme and parsley.

Let simmer for 10 minutes over low heat and add the fish or chicken stock, Chicoutai liqueur and maple syrup. Cover and continue cooking for 10 minutes over low heat.

Add the mussels, shrimp, scallops, salmon and clams. Cover and simmer for 2 minutes over low heat; season.

Serve in soup bowls and garnish with chopped fresh parsley.

COLD AND CREAMY SMOKED SALMON SOUP

4 SERVINGS

Preparation Time: 10 minutes

Cooking Time: 20 minutes

2	large potatoes, peeled and diced
1	leek, sliced
1	onion, sliced
2 cups	(500 ml) chicken stock, skimmed of fat
1 cup	(250 ml) milk
1 cup	(250 ml) sour cream
3/4 cup	(175 ml) coarsely cut smoked salmon
1 tbsp	(15 ml) lemon juice
	salt and pepper
1/3 cup	(75 ml) smoked salmon, cut in strips
2	green onions, sliced

In a pot, combine the potatoes, leeks and onion. Add the chicken stock and the milk. Bring to a boil, cover and cook over low heat for 20 minutes.

Pour the mixture into a large bowl. Add the sour cream, chopped smoked salmon and lemon juice. Reduce to a smooth purée using an electric mixer; season.

Cover and refrigerate for at least 4 hours. When ready to serve, pour into chilled soup bowls, and garnish with strips of smoked salmon and green onion.

CREAM OF FENNEL SOUP WITH SNOW CRAB

4 TO 6 SERVINGS

Preparation Time: 15 minutes

Cooking Time: 30 minutes

1 tbsp	(15 ml) butter
1/2 cup	(125 ml) coarsely chopped onions
1/2 cup	(125 ml) chopped celery
1/2 cup	(125 ml) chopped leeks
1	fennel bulb, leaves removed and chopped
1 cup	(250 ml) diced potatoes
1	sprig of parsley
5 cups	(1.25 L) chicken stock, skimmed of fat
	salt and pepper, to taste
1/2 cup	(125 ml) 15% cream
1/2 cup	(125 ml) snow crab

In a large pot, melt the butter and sauté the onions, celery, leeks and fennel.

Add the potatoes, parsley and chicken stock. Let simmer for 25 minutes and season.

Purée using a food processor or an electric mixer. Return to the saucepan and reheat.

When ready to serve, add the cream and snow crab. Serve hot and garnish with fennel leaves, if desired.

SEAFOOD WRAPS WITH LOBSTER COULIS

8 SERVINGS

Preparation Time: 20 minutes
Cooking Time: 30 minutes

- 1 onion, diced
- 1 celery stalk, diced
- 1 small leek, diced
- **1 tbsp** (15 ml) corn oil
- **1 lb** (500 g) lobster cut into pieces
- **2 tbsp** (25 ml) tomato paste
- **1 cup** (250 ml) dry white wine
- **1 cup** (250 ml) water or fish stock
- 1 bay leaf
- 1 stalk of thyme
- 1 sprig of parsley
- **2 tbsp** (25 ml) chopped, fresh tarragon
- salt and pepper, to taste
- **4 tbsp** (60 ml) corn starch or flour
- **2 tbsp** (25 ml) butter
- **1/4 lb** (125 g) fresh scallops
- **1/4 lb** (125 g) Nordic shrimp
- 4 sheets of philo pastry
- 1 pie plate
- 4 clusters of fresh tarragon

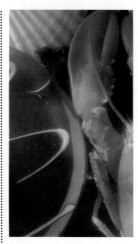

Preheat the oven to 400°F (200°C).

In a large saucepan, heat the oil over medium heat. Sauté the lobster, onion, celery and leek for approximately 10 minutes. Add the tomato paste, white wine and water. Add the spices and tarragon. Let simmer for 10 minutes. Season with salt and pepper, to taste.

Remove the vegetables and lobster from the pan. Shell the lobster, and set aside the meat. Thicken the sauce with cornstarch or flour and keep warm over low heat.

In a non-stick pan, melt the butter and lightly sauté the scallops for approximately 2 minutes. Remove from the stove and mix with the shrimp, lobster meat and 2 tbsp (25 ml) of lobster coulis. Mix well.

Spread 2 sheets of philo pastry on a flat surface and lightly brush with melted butter. Cover with the other two sheets. Cut them into four equal parts and brush again with butter. This process must be done quickly, as the philo may become dry. Place an adequate amount of the seafood preparation on each of the pieces of pastry and roll into the form of a log. Repeat this procedure with the remaining pastry.

SCALLOP SALAD WITH CHIVES

4 SERVINGS

Preparation Time: 15 minutes

Cooking Time: 5 minutes

6 cups	(1.5 L) of assorted lettuce (radicchio, watercress, Boston, etc…)
1/4 cup	(50 ml) olive oil
1/2 lb	(250 g) scallops
	salt and pepper, to taste
2 tsp	(10 ml) balsamic vinegar
1 tbsp	(15 ml) lemon juice
1 tsp	(5 ml) lime juice
2 tbsp	(25 ml) finely chopped chives
1	tomato, seeded and diced
8	whole chives

Line the center of the serving plates with lettuce and set aside.

In a pan, heat the oil over medium heat and cook the scallops for 1 to 2 minutes on each side (depending on the size); season.

Add the vinegar, lemon juice and lime juice. Let simmer for 1 minute and add the chopped chives.

Arrange the scallops on the lettuce lined plates and drizzle the vinaigrette over the top. Garnish with diced tomatoes and whole chives.

HAWAIIAN STYLE FISHERMAN SALAD

4 SERVINGS

Preparation Time: 20 minutes

Cooking Time: none

1 lb	(500 g) cooked white fish (sole, cod or seabass) cut into strips
1 1/2 cups	(375 ml) shrimp
3 tbsp	(50 ml) lime juice
1	green onion, chopped
2 tbsp	(25 ml) mayonnaise
3/4 cup	(175 ml) coconut milk
1	pink grapefruit, peeled and cut into wedges
1	orange, peeled and cut into wedges
1	tomato, seeded, peeled and diced
2 tbsp	(25 ml) capers, drained
8	leaves of curly red lettuce or other mixed greens

GARNISH

A few whole chives

In a large bowl, mix together the fish, shrimp, lime juice, green onion, mayonnaise and coconut milk. Cover and let set in the refrigerator for 2 to 4 hours.

Add the grapefruit, orange, diced tomatoes and capers to the fish mixture.

Line four plates with lettuce and arrange the fish mixture in the center. Garnish with whole chives.

SUMMER SHELL SALAD

4 SERVINGS

Preparation Time: 20 minutes

Cooking Time: 5 minutes

1 tsp	(5 ml) Dijon mustard
1/3 cup	(75 ml) olive oil
1 tbsp	(15 ml) vinegar (balsamic, red wine, white wine or regular)
1 tbsp	(15 ml) lemon juice
	salt and pepper, to taste
4 oz	(125 g) cooked shell pasta
1	avocado, peeled, pitted and cubed
1	tomato, seeded and diced
1/2	cucumber cut into thin, semicircular slices
4 oz	(125 g) small Nordic shrimp
4	cauliflower florets, blanched
12	snowpeas, blanched
2 tbsp	(25 ml) finely chopped parsley
4	lettuce leaves

GARNISH

1/2 cup	(125 ml) grated carrot
4	bunches of alfalfa sprouts

In a large bowl, mix together the Dijon mustard, olive oil, vinegar and lemon juice; season.

Add the shell pasta, avocado, tomato, cucumber, shrimp, cauliflower, snowpeas and parsley. Mix well.

Serve on a bed of lettuce, garnish with grated carrots and alfalfa.

FRUITY SMOKED SALMON SALAD

4 SERVINGS

Preparation Time: 15 minutes

Cooking Time: 10 minutes

1/2 lb	(250 g) mixed green lettuce
1	orange, peeled and thinly sliced
1	red onion, finely chopped
2	apples, thinly sliced
8	slices of smoked salmon, cut into strips
1/2	pomegranate

VINAIGRETTE

1 1/2 cups	(375 ml) apple juice
1 tbsp	(15 ml) raspberry vinegar
1/4 cup	(50 ml) olive oil
	ground cinnamon, to taste
	salt and pepper, to taste

In a saucepan, bring the apple juice to a boil, and let reduce by one third. Let cool. In a bowl, combine all the ingredients of the vinaigrette, add the juice and mix.

Line a serving platter with the mixed greens, orange, onions, and apples. Dress with the vinaigrette.

Before serving, place the smoked salmon on the top and garnish with the pomegranate grains.

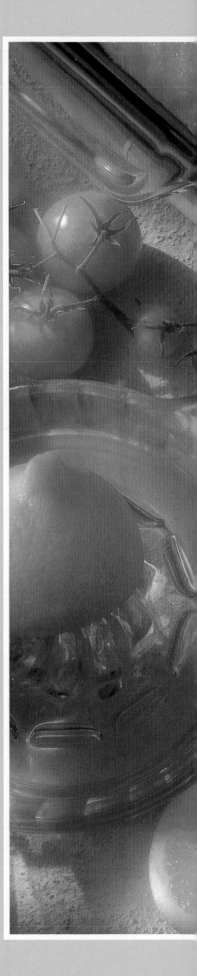

SMOKED SALMON WITH HERB DRESSING

4 SERVINGS
Preparation Time: 20 minutes
Cooking Time: 30 minutes

- **1/2 lb** (250 g) smoked salmon
- **1/2 cup** (125 ml) leek julienned
- **1 cup** (250 ml) carrots, julienned
- **1** green onion, chopped
- **1/2** green pepper, sliced

HERB DRESSING
- **1 cup** (250 ml) plain yogurt
- **2 tbsp** (25 ml) lemon juice
- **1/4 cup** (50 ml) mustard
- **1/4 cup** (50 ml) salted herbs

GARNISH
- **4** leaves of curly lettuce
- **4** cherry tomatoes or quartered tomatoes
- **4** slices of lemon
- **1/2 cup** (125 ml) alfalfa

In a large bowl, mix together the ingredients of the herb dressing.

Cut the smoked salmon into thin strips. Blanch the leeks and carrots in salted, boiling water. Let cool.

Add the smoked salmon, leeks, carrots, onion and green pepper to the herb dressing; mix well.

Line the plates with lettuce and place the smoked salmon mixture on top.

Garnish with tomatoes, lemon slices and alfalfa.

AVOCADO SALAD WITH LOBSTER AND GRAPEFRUIT

6 SERVINGS

Preparation Time: 25 minutes
Cooking Time: none

ROSÉ VINAIGRETTE WITH GINGER

1 cup	(250 ml) yogurt
2 tbsp	(25 ml) chopped, fresh chives or green onions
1/2 tsp	(2 ml) finely chopped fresh ginger
1 tbsp	(15 ml) chili sauce
1/2 tsp	(2 ml) tabasco sauce
1/2 tsp	(2 ml) paprika
1 tbsp	(15 ml) honey
2 tsp	(10 ml) lemon juice

SALAD

2	peeled avocados, cut in half (lengthwise) lemon juice
2 or 3	pink grapefruits (cut into wedges)
1	pack of frozen lobster meat or fresh lobster
1	head of lettuce
1 cup	(250 ml) sliced mushrooms

VINAIGRETTE

Mix together all the ingredients of the vinaigrette. Cover and refrigerate for 1 to 2 hours.

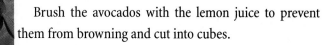

SALAD

Brush the avocados with the lemon juice to prevent them from browning and cut into cubes.

Garnish the plates as follows: arrange the avocado, grapefruit, and lobster in rows on a bed of lettuce, alternating, so as to show only a border of lettuce. Dress with the vinaigrette. Garnish with mushrooms.

MAPLE SCALLOPS

4 SERVINGS

Preparation Time: 15 minutes
Cooking Time: 15 minutes

1 tsp	(5 ml) ground cumin
1 tsp	(5 ml) ground curry
1/2 tsp	(2 ml) ground coriander seeds
1 tbsp	(15 ml) maple sugar
2 tbsp	(25 ml) olive oil
1	green onion, sliced
24	scallops
1 tbsp	(15 ml) butter
2	green onions, sliced
2 cups	(500 ml) watercress leaves
1/2 cup	(125 ml) chicken stock, skimmed of fat
1/2 cup	(125 ml) 35% cream
1 tsp	(5 ml) all-purpose flour
1 tsp	(5 ml) butter
	salt and pepper, to taste
4	sprigs of watercress
4	cherry tomatoes

In a bowl, mix together the cumin, curry, ground coriander seeds, maple sugar, olive oil, green onion and scallops. Marinate for 1 to 2 hours in the refrigerator.

In a saucepan, melt the butter and lightly sauté the onions and watercress. Add the chicken stock and cream. Let simmer for 1 to 2 minutes over low heat and thicken with a mixture of flour and butter; season to taste. Purée in a food processor, and then return to the saucepan.

Preheat the oven to 400°F (200°C). Bake the scallops for 3 to 5 minutes(depending on their size),turning halfway through the cooking time.

Line the serving plates with creamed watercress and then garnish with the scallops. Garnish with sprigs of watercress and cherry tomatoes.

If scallop shells are available, one may wish to present the scallops in the shell, as shown in the picture.

LOBSTER AU GRATIN

4 SERVINGS

Preparation Time: 10 minutes

Cooking Time: 8 to 10 minutes

2	slices of white bread, with the crusts removed
1/2 cup	(125 ml) warm milk
2 tbsp	(25 ml) butter
4	shallots, finely chopped
1	garlic clove, minced
3 cups	(750 ml) cooked and chopped lobster meat
1/2 cup	(125 ml) grated Parmesan cheese
	salt and pepper, to taste
1 cup	(250 ml) toasted breadcrumbs
1	pinch of Cayenne pepper

Preheat the oven to 400°F (200°C). In a bowl, dip the bread in the warm milk and set aside.

In a pan, melt the butter over medium heat and sauté the shallots and the garlic. Remove from the stove and add the dampened bread, the lobster meat and Parmesan cheese. Season and mix well.

Transfer the mixture to four greased, ovenproof plates and sprinkle with breadcrumbs and Cayenne pepper. Bake for 8 to 10 minutes or until the top is golden. Serve hot.

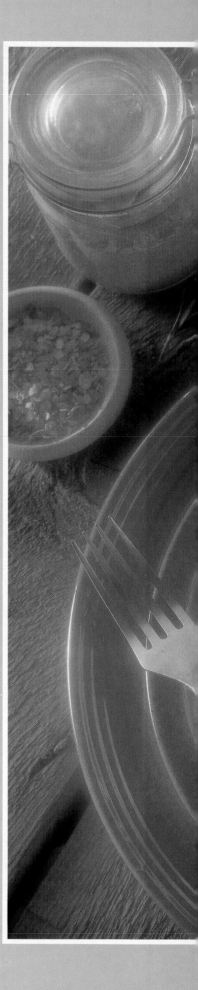

BATTERED MONKFISH WITH TOMATO COULIS

4 SERVINGS

Preparation Time: 30 minutes
Cooking Time: 25 minutes

2 tbsp (25 ml) butter
3/4 lb (350 g) monkfish cut into 1 1/2
in (3 cm) cubes
1 garlic clove, minced
corn oil for frying
GARNISH
1 stalk of fresh thyme
BATTER
1/2 cup (125 ml) all-purpose flour
2 medium egg yolks
1 tsp (5 ml) salt
1 cup (250 ml) milk
2 medium egg whites, whisked to
form soft peaks
TOMATO COULIS
2 tbsp (25 ml) corn oil
1/2 cup (125 ml) sliced onions
5 tomatoes, peeled,
seeded and cubed
1 tsp (5 ml) chopped, fresh thyme
1 bay leaf
1/2 cup (125 ml) dry white wine

Melt the butter in a saucepan over low heat. Add the monkfish and garlic cover half the pan and let steam for approximately 10 minutes. Remove from heat and let cool.

BATTER

In a large mixing bowl, whisk together the flour, egg yolks, salt and milk. Add the egg whites.

Dip the monkfish cubes into the batter and fry until golden. Drain on paper towel.

TOMATO COULIS

In a saucepan, heat the oil and sauté the onions and tomatoes, adding the thyme and bay leaf. Add the white wine and let simmer over low heat for 10 minutes. Remove the bay leaf and purée the remaining mixture using an electric mixer or food processor. Pour over the monkfish and garnish with a stalk of fresh thyme.

MUSSELS MARINARA WITH FRESH BASIL

4 SERVINGS

Preparation Time: 20 minutes
Cooking Time: 10 minutes

2 lbs (1 kg) mussels
1/4 cup (50 ml) olive oil
1/4 cup (50 ml) chopped shallots
1 tsp (5 ml) minced garlic
1 cup (250 ml) dry white wine or
chicken stock, skimmed of fat
28 oz (796 ml) tomatoes with fine herbs
peeled and crushed
1/2 cup (125 ml) chopped, fresh basil
2 tbsp (25 ml) chopped, fresh parsley
salt and pepper, to taste
2 tsp (10 ml) cornstarch, diluted in
a little water
4 sprigs of fresh basil or parsley

Clean and debeard the mussels in cold water.

In a large saucepan, heat the oil and lightly brown the shallots. Add the garlic, mussels, white wine, tomatoes, basil and parsley; season. Cover and let simmer for 5 minutes, or until the mussels are open. Discard any mussels that do not open.

Place the mussels in a serving dish. Thicken the sauce with cornstarch, diluted in a little water. Pour the sauce over the mussels. Garnish with sprigs of basil and serve.

SALMON & SHRIMP SAVARINS

4 TO 6 SERVINGS

Preparation Time: 15 minutes

Cooking Time: 30 minutes

6 oz (180 g) fresh salmon fillets, deboned
1 egg white
1/2 cup (125 ml) 35% cream
   salt and pepper, to taste
3/4 lb (375 g) small shrimp, warm
2 tbsp (25 ml) diced tomato or red pepper
GARNISH
6 sprigs of fresh basil
CREAM SAUCE
1 tbsp (15 ml) butter
2 tbsp (25 ml) chopped shallots
1 tsp (5 ml) all-purpose flour
1/2 cup (125 ml) dry white wine
1 cup (250 ml) fish stock
1/2 cup (125 ml) 35% cream
   salt and pepper, to taste
2 tbsp (25 ml) chopped, fresh basil

Preheat the oven to 300°F (160°C). In a food processor, mix together the salmon and the egg white. While mixing, slowly add the cream; season.

Place the mixture in the savarins molds or in a greased muffin pan. Bake in the oven, slightly submerged in water, for 15 to 20 minutes. Remove from the molds and keep warm.

CREAM SAUCE

In a saucepan, melt the butter and lightly sauté the shallots. Sprinkle with flour and stir. Add the white wine, fish stock and cream; season. Cook for 5 minutes, while stirring.

Strain and keep warm.

When ready to serve, add the basil to the sauce and line the bottoms of the serving plates. Place the salmon savarins and the shrimp on the plates. Pour a little sauce over the shrimp. Garnish with diced tomatoes and sprigs of basil.

ESCARGOTS WITH MIGNERON CHEESE

4 SERVINGS

Preparation Time: 15 minutes

Cooking Time: 5 minutes

3 tbsp	(50 ml) butter
40	escargots (snails)
3	shallots, chopped
	salt and pepper, to taste
1 3/4 cups	(425 ml) white wine
20	quail eggs
	salt and pepper, to taste
	chopped chives, to taste
3/4 cup	(175 ml) 35% cream
	(per person)
8	thin slices of Migneron cheese

In a saucepan, melt the butter and sauté the escargots with the shallots, salt and pepper. Add the white wine and let reduce.

Break the eggs, in groups of five, beat together with the cream. Season and add the chives. Cook the mixture as you would scrambled eggs.

Garnish with two slices of Migneron cheese. Serve with a small salad.

For each additional person, add 10 escargots, five quail eggs and a little cream.

STUFFED PHILO

4 SERVINGS

Preparation Time: 20 minutes

Cooking Time: 25 minutes

1	small onion, chopped
2	green onions, chopped
1 cup	(250 ml) chopped celery
1/2 cup	(125 ml) chopped carrots
1 cup	(250 ml) sliced mushrooms
1	garlic clove, minced
1 cup	(250 ml) cooked shrimps
1/2 cup	(125 ml) diced, cooked ham
2 tbsp	(25 ml) chopped, fresh parsley
1	egg, beaten
	pepper, to taste
4	sheets of philo pastry

Preheat the oven to 375°F (190°C). Spray the inside of a saucepan with cooking spray and sauté the onions, celery, carrots, mushrooms and garlic for 3 to 5 minutes.

Add the shrimp, ham and parsley and let the mixture cool.

Add the egg and season to taste.

Brush each sheet of philo pastry with water. Transfer the vegetable mix and shrimp to the middle of the sheet and roll up.

Place on a cookie sheet and bake for 20 minutes. when ready to serve, cut each philo roll into slices.

WATER LILY FLAKY PASTRY

4 SERVINGS

Preparation Time: 15 minutes
Cooking Time: 20 minutes

16	large frog legs, blanched
4 oz	(125 g) flaky pastry dough
1 tbsp	(15 ml) butter
2 tbsp	(25 ml) chopped shallots
	salt and pepper, to taste
1 cup	(250 ml) dry white wine or
	chicken stock, skimmed of fat
1 cup	(250 ml) 35% cream
2 tsp	(10 ml) white sauce thickener
2 tbsp	(25 ml) chopped chives
2 tbsp	(25 ml) chopped, fresh parsley
2 tbsp	(25 ml) chopped, fresh basil or
1 tsp	(5 ml) dry basil
GLAZE	
1	egg
1 tbsp	(15 ml) milk

On a cutting board, debone the frog legs and reserve the meat.

Preheat the oven to 375°F (190°C). Roll out the flaky pastry dough and cut into 3.5 in (9 cm) diameter circles. Place the pastry dough on a greased cookie sheet and brush with the glaze (a mixture of the milk and egg). Bake for 10 to 12 minutes or until the dough is golden.

In a saucepan, melt the butter and sauté the shallots and the frog legs. Season and add the white wine or chicken stock. Let simmer for 1 to 2 minutes.

Remove the frog legs and keep warm. Add the cream to the sauce and thicken with a little sauce thickener. Strain the sauce and keep warm. Add the herbs

Cut each flaky pastry in half horizontally and garnish the bottom part with the frog legs. Cover with sauce and close with the top part of the flaky pastry.

MINI VOL-AU-VENT WITH ESCARGOTS

4 SERVINGS

Preparation Time: 10 minutes
Cooking Time: 15 minutes

2 tbsp	(25 ml) butter
24	escargots (snails)
2 tbsp	(25 ml) chopped shallots
2 tbsp	(25 ml) chopped, fresh parsley
1/3 cup	(75 ml) Kalhua liqueur
1 cup	(250 ml) 35% cream
2 tbsp	(25 ml) chopped, fresh tarragon
	or 1 tsp (5 ml) dry tarragon
	salt and pepper, to taste
4	mini vol-au-vent, warm
4	sprigs of fresh tarragon or parsley
1	tomato, seeded and diced

In a saucepan, melt the butter and sauté the escargots for 1 minute over medium heat. Add the shallots and parsley.

Add the Kalhua and incorporate the cream. Let reduce until the sauce thickens. Add the tarragon and season to taste.

Place the mini vol-au-vent in the center of the serving plates and garnish with the escargots. Garnish with the sprigs of tarragon and diced tomatoes.

RED SNAPPER WITH CHIVE SAUCE

4 SERVINGS

Preparation Time: 10 minutes
Cooking Time: 25 minutes

1/3 cup	(75 ml) butter
1/2 cup	(125 ml) chopped chives
1/2 cup	(125 ml) 35% cream
1 cup	(250 ml) butter, cut into pieces
	salt and pepper, to taste
1 cup	(250 ml) fish stock or
	chicken stock, skimmed of fat
4	5 oz (150 g) red snapper fillets

GARNISH

8	whole chives

In a saucepan, melt the butter and incorporate the chives. Cook for 5 to 7 minutes over very low heat.

Add the cream, cook over medium heat and reduce by 75%. Strain the sauce into another saucepan.

Put back on the stove over low heat and add pieces of butter, one by one, while constantly whipping the mixture. Keep warm and season to taste.

In a buttered saucepan, bring the fish stock to a boil. Poach the red snapper, covered, for 5 minutes.

Serve the red snapper covered in cream sauce. Garnish with whole chives and fresh vegetables.

TROUT WITH LIME

4 SERVINGS

Preparation Time: 10 minutes
Cooking Time: 7 minutes

1 tbsp	(15 ml) melted butter
1/2	onion, finely chopped
8	trout fillets
	ground pepper, to taste
	juice of 2 limes

In a pan, melt the butter and lightly sauté the onions for 2 minutes.

Add the trout fillets, season and baste with the lime juice. Let simmer for 7 minutes. Serve.

SALMON HOT POT

4 SERVINGS
Preparation Time: 20 minutes
Cooking Time: 20 minutes

1 lb	(450 g) chopped vegetables (turnips, rutabaga, potatoes, fresh peas, zucchini and carrots)
2 cups	(500 ml) fish stock, skimmed of fat
1 1/2 lb	(575 g) salmon, cut into round pieces
1/4 cup	(50 ml) salt spice (thyme, savory, lavanche, a bay leaf, nutmeg, parsley)

GARNISH

4	stalks of marjoram

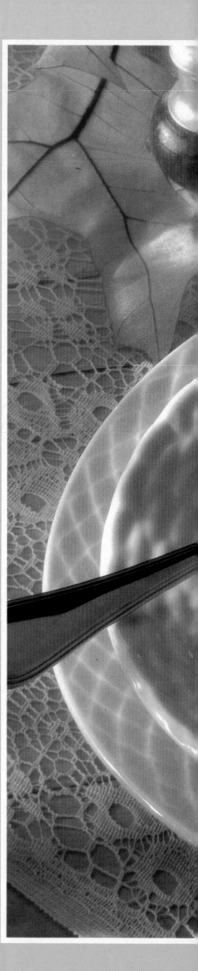

In a saucepan, cook the vegetables in the fish stock until the vegetables are still slightly crisp. Drain and keep the cooking juice.

Return the cooking juice to the saucepan and add the salmon. Cover and let simmer until the salmon is cooked. Add the salt spice halfway through the cooking time. Remove the salmon from the pan and set aside.

Reduce the cooking juice until you have 1 cup (250 ml) left. Put the salmon and vegetables back in the pan and reheat slowly.

Divide the vegetables into four equal parts and place on deep serving plates.

Place the salmon in the center of each plate.

Dress with the cooking juice and garnish with stalks of marjoram.

BOUILLABAISSE WITH SPICY CROUTONS

4 SERVINGS

Preparation Time: 30 minutes
Cooking Time: 15 minutes

1/3 cup	(75 ml) olive oil
1/2 cup	(125 ml) chopped onion
1/2 cup	(125 ml) chopped leek
2	garlic cloves, minced
2	potatoes, peeled and diced
1 tbsp	(15 ml) chopped fennel
2 tbsp	(25 ml) chopped, fresh parsley
1 tsp	(5 ml) chopped, fresh savory
1	bay leaf
1	pinch of saffron
1 lb	(500 g) monkfish cut into pieces
1 lb	(500 g) red snapper cut into pieces (you may substitute with fresh fish)
12	shrimps, cooked and shelled
12	scallops
8	clams, left in their shells
12	mussels, left in their shells
1 lb	(500 g) lobster, cooked and shelled
2	fresh tomatoes, peeled, seeded and diced
1/4 cup	(50 ml) cognac or brandy
1/2 cup	(125 ml) dry white wine
6 cups	(1.5 L) water
	salt and pepper, to taste

SPICY CROUTONS

3	garlic cloves
2	slices of white bread, crusts removed
1	pinch of saffron
3-6 drops	Tabasco
	salt and pepper, to taste
1/4 cup	(50 ml) olive oil
12	pieces of thinly sliced, baguette (French bread)

In a large pot, heat the olive oil over medium heat and sauté the onion, leeks, garlic and potatoes. Add the fennel, parsley, savory, bay leaf and saffron.

Incorporate the fish, shrimps, scallops, clams, mussels and lobster meat. Add the tomatoes, cognac, white wine and water; season. Cover and cook over high heat for 6 to 8 minutes.

SPICY CROUTONS

With a food processor or an electric mixer, mix together all the ingredients with the exception of the baguette slices, until a smooth texture is reached. Spread the paste on the slices of bread and place on a cookie sheet. Lightly brown in the oven, set on broil.

Serve the bouillabaisse in large soup bowls and garnish with croutons. Serve the remaining spread on the side.

TUNA BROCHETTES WITH ANISETTE

4 SERVINGS

Preparation Time: 15 minutes
Cooking Time: 10 minutes

2 tbsp	(25 ml) corn oil
	juice of 1 lemon
1/2 tsp	(2 ml) curry powder
1 tsp	(5 ml) chopped, fresh thyme
1/4 cup	(50 ml) Anisette liqueur
8	mushrooms
1	zucchini cut into semicircles (28 pieces)
1 1/2 lb	(750 g) tuna cut into 1 in (2.5 cm) cubes
	salt and pepper, to taste

In a bowl, mix together, the oil, lemon juice, curry powder, thyme and the Anisette liqueur.

Using skewers, thread a mushroom, followed by a piece of zucchini and a cube of tuna. Repeat to obtain seven cubes of tuna and seven pieces of zucchini on each skewer. Finish with a mushroom.

Place the brochettes in a baking dish and pour the marinade over the brochettes. Marinate for 15 minutes at room temperature.

Set the oven to broil. Remove the brochettes from the marinade, place on a cookie sheet and season. Broil for 5 minutes, turning halfway through the cooking time. Serve on a bed of rice, with lemon seasoned vegetables.

SALMON FILLETS WITH BARLEY

4 SERVINGS

Preparation Time: 15 minutes
Cooking Time: 1 hour

2 tsp	(10 ml) butter
2 tbsp	(25 ml) chopped shallots
1 cup	(250 ml) barley
12 oz	(341 ml) beer
1 cup	(250 ml) chicken stock
1 tbsp	(15 ml) chopped, fresh parsley
	salt and pepper, to taste
2 tsp	(10 ml) butter
8	salmon fillets
1 tbsp	(15 ml) chopped shallots
1 cup	(250 ml) beer
1 cup	(250 ml) melted butter
1 tsp	(5 ml) flour
1 tsp	(5 ml) chopped chives
1	tomato, seeded and diced

In a saucepan, melt the butter and lightly sauté the shallots.

Add the barley, beer, chicken stock and parsley; season. Cover and let simmer over low heat, for approximately 45 minutes. Keep warm.

In a large frying pan, melt the butter and cook the salmon with the shallots for 1 minute on each side. Season to taste.

Remove the fillets from the frying pan and keep warm. Pour the beer and chicken stock into the frying pan. Reduce by half and slightly thicken with a mixture of butter and flour.

Serve the salmon on a bed of barley. Cover with sauce, and garnish with chives and diced tomatoes.

SALMON FILLETS WITH LEEK SAUCE

2 SERVINGS

Preparation Time: 30 minutes
Cooking Time: 15 to 20 minutes

2	fresh salmon fillets, approximately 5 1/2 oz (150 g) each juice of 1/2 lemon

LEEK SAUCE

2	medium shallots or green onions, sliced
1 tbsp	(15 ml) butter
1/3 cup	(75 ml) dry white vermouth or white wine
1/2 cup	(125 ml) beef or chicken stock, skimmed of fat
1/2 cup	(125 ml) 35% cream
1	leek stalk, julienned
2 tbsp	(25 ml) fresh coriander
1	pinch of Cayenne pepper

GARNISH

	sprig of dill or stalk of tarragon

Preheat the oven to 350°F (180°C). Grease two ovenproof plates and set aside. Slice each salmon fillet horizontally, reducing its thickness by half and making sure not to puncture the skin. Open and place each salmon fillet between two sheets of plastic wrap and gently flatten with the flat part of a knife.

Place onto the two greased plates. Squeeze lemon juice over each fillet.

LEEK SAUCE

In a saucepan, over medium-high heat, cook the shallots in butter for a few minutes. Add the dry vermouth and reduce until only 1 tbsp (15 ml) of liquid remains.

Add the stock and reduce by 1/3. Add the 35% cream and reduce again. Add the leeks, coriander, and Cayenne pepper. Simmer over low heat for 3 to 4 minutes.

Bake the salmon for 8 to 10 minutes. When serving, pour the salmon sauce over the salmon and garnish with dill or tarragon.

FILLET OF SOLE

4 SERVINGS

Preparation Time: 20 minutes
Cooking Time: 10 minutes

	ground pepper, to taste
	all-purpose flour
8	fresh or frozen sole fillets, 3 1/2 oz (100 g) each
1 tbsp	(15 ml) olive oil
2 tbsp	(25 ml) capers, drained
2	lemons, peeled and cut in wedges
2 tbsp	(25 ml) finely chopped black olives
1/4 cup	(50 ml) dry white wine
1/4 cup	(50 ml) croutons
1 tbsp	(15 ml) chopped, fresh parsley

Season and coat the sole fillets with flour. Heat the oil in a non-stick pan and sear the sole fillets over medium-high heat for 2 to 3 minutes on each side or until lightly golden. Remove from the pan and set aside.

Using the same pan, lightly sauté the capers, lemon wedges and black olives, then add the dry white wine. Let simmer for 3 to 4 minutes over low heat, and return the sole to the pan. Add the croutons and parsley.

When serving pour the sauce over the sole fillets.

SEABASS WITH TOMATO COULIS

4 SERVINGS

Preparation Time: 15 minutes
Cooking Time: 35 minutes

19 oz	(540 ml) tomatoes with fine herbs
1 tbsp	(15 ml) corn oil
1/4 cup	(50 ml) chopped onion
1 tbsp	(15 ml) chopped, fresh garlic
	salt and pepper, to taste
1 1/2 lb	(750 g) seabass fillets (or perch)
4	aluminum foil sheets

Preheat the oven to 375°F (190°C).

With a hand mixer, crush the tomatoes and set aside.

In a pan, heat the oil and lightly brown the onions. Add the garlic and tomatoes; season. Simmer over low heat for 20 minutes and set aside.

Place the seabass fillets on the 4 sheets of aluminum foil. Pour the tomato sauce over the fillets.

Fold the aluminum foil over the fillets and close tightly. Place on a cookie sheet and bake for approximately 12 minutes.

FILLET OF SOLE IN MUSHROOM SAUCE

4 SERVINGS

Preparation Time: 10 minutes
Cooking Time: 15 minutes

1 tbsp	(15 ml) butter
2 tbsp	(25 ml) chopped shallots
1 1/2 lb	(750 g) fillet of sole
	salt and pepper, to taste
1 cup	(250 ml) dry white wine
1/2 cup	(125 ml) 15% cream
2 tbsp	(25 ml) white sauce thickener
2 tbsp	(25 ml) butter
1 1/2 cups	(375 ml) sliced mushrooms

In a frying pan, melt the butter and lightly sauté the shallots. Place the sole in the frying pan and season. Add the white wine, cover and poach for 5 minutes. Be careful not to over cook.

Remove the fillets from the frying pan and keep warm. Incorporate the cream to the frying pan and let simmer for 2 minutes. Thicken with white sauce thickener. Strain the sauce and keep warm.

In another frying pan, melt the butter and lightly sauté the mushrooms. Drain and add to the sauce. Pour the mushroom sauce over the fish and serve.

SALMON MILLE-FEUILLES

4 SERVINGS

Preparation Time: 30 minutes
Cooking Time: 20 minutes

BUTTER SAUCE
- **1 cup** (250 ml) dry white wine
- **2 tbsp** (25 ml) chopped shallots
- **1/4 cup** (50 ml) 35% cream
- **1 1/2 cups** (375 ml) butter, cut in pieces
- **1/2 cup** (125 ml) chopped, fresh basil or 1 tsp (5 ml) dried basil
  salt and pepper, to taste

SALMON MILLE-FEUILLES
- **2 tsp** (10 ml) olive oil
- **12** salmon fillets, 2 oz.(60 g) each
  salt and pepper, to taste
- **1** package of spinach, washed, blanched and warm
- **1** small leek, washed, finely chopped, blanched and warm
- **2** tomatoes, peeled and diced
- **1/3 cup** (75 ml) 15% cream

GARNISH
- **1/4 cup** (50 ml) caviar
- **1** tomato, peeled and diced
  zest of 1 lemon
- **4** sprigs of fresh basil

BUTTER SAUCE

In a saucepan, mix together the wine and the shallots and cook over medium heat. Reduce by two thirds. Add the cream and reduce until only 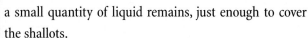 a small quantity of liquid remains, just enough to cover the shallots.

Incorporate the pieces of butter, one at a time, while whipping vigorously. Add the basil, season and mix. Keep warm over low heat.

SALMON MILLE-FEUILLES

In a large pan, heat the oil and cook the salmon fillets for 1 minute on each side; season.

Place the salmon on a greased cookie sheet and cover with half of the spinach. Place another salmon fillet over the top and cover with the leeks. Finish with another layer of salmon. Sprinkle with diced tomatoes and brown in the oven, set on broil, for approximately 1 minute.

Line the plates with the butter sauce; set aside.

With a food processor or an electric mixer, reduce the remaining spinach to a purée, adding the 35% cream. Pour into a pastry bag and make zigzags on the bottom of the plates. Place a salmon mille-feuille in the center of each plate.

Garnish with caviar, diced tomatoes, lemon zest and fresh basil.

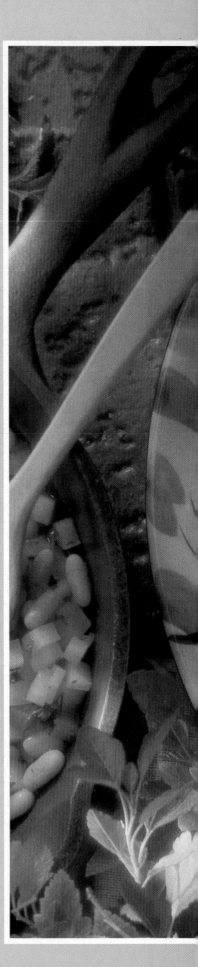
HALIBUT STEAKS WITH KIDNEY BEANS

4 SERVINGS

Preparation Time: 15 minutes
Cooking Time: 30 minutes

1 tsp	(5 ml) chopped onion
1/2 cup	(125 ml) diced celery
1 cup	(250 ml) diced turnip
1 cup	(250 ml) diced carrot
1 tsp	(5 ml) minced garlic
2	tomatoes, diced
1 1/2 cups	(375 ml) chicken stock, skimmed of fat
12 oz	(341 ml) kidney beans
1 tbsp	(15 ml) chopped, fresh parsley
2 tbsp	(25 ml) chopped, fresh chervil
	or 1 tsp (5 ml) dried chervil
	salt and pepper, to taste
1 tsp	(5 ml) corn oil
1 tsp	(5 ml) butter
4	halibut steaks, 5 oz (150 g) each

Preheat the oven to 350°F (180°C). In a non-stick pan, lightly brown the onion, celery, turnip and carrots.

Add the garlic, tomatoes, chicken stock, kidney beans, parsley and chervil. Season and simmer over medium heat for 5 minutes. Reduce the heat and keep warm.

In another frying pan, heat the oil and butter over medium heat. Pan sear the halibut steaks for 2 minutes on each side. Season to taste.

Place the kidney beans in a baking dish. Place the halibut steaks over the beans and bake for 15 minutes.

SALMON WITH BEURRE BLANC AND BABY VEGETABLES

4 SERVINGS

Preparation Time: 25 minutes
Cooking Time: 15 minutes

4	salmon fillets
	salt and pepper, to taste
1/4 cup	(50 ml) butter
1 cup	(250 ml) carrot, julienned
1 cup	(250 ml) celery, julienned
1 cup	(250 ml) zucchini, julienned
1 cup	(250 ml) mushrooms, cut in quarters

BEURRE BLANC

3	shallots, finely chopped
1/2 cup	(125 ml) dry white wine
1/4 cup	(50 ml) 35% cream
	salt and pepper, to taste
1 cup	(250 ml) softened butter

Season the salmon. In an ovenproof skillet, melt the butter over medium heat and cook the salmon on both sides. Remove from the frying pan.

Add the vegetables and sauté over high heat for 2 to 3 minutes. Place the salmon on top of the vegetables and bake at 350°F (180°C) for 5 to 7 minutes.

Prepare the butter sauce by combining the shallots and white wine in a saucepan. Bring to a boil and reduce until the saucepan is almost dry.

Add the cream and season. Remove from heat and gradually add the butter while stirring vigorously.

Place the vegetables on plates, and place the salmon fillets on top. Pour the butter sauce over the fillets.

TROUT WITH HAM

4 SERVINGS

Preparation Time: 25 minutes
Cooking Time: 20 minutes

4	rainbow trout, cleaned
8	slices of ham
1/3 cup	(75 ml) butter
1 cup	(250 ml) thinly sliced mushrooms
1 cup	(250 ml) cubed leeks
2	slices of ham, cut into strips
	salt and pepper, to taste
1/2 cup	(125 ml) dry white wine
1/2 cup	(125 ml) 35% cream

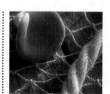

Roll the trout in slices of Bayonne ham. In a non-stick pan, melt the butter over medium high heat and cook the trout for 5 minutes on each side. Remove and set aside.

In the same pan, sauté the mushrooms for 5 minutes. Add the leek and ham; season and add the white wine. Let simmer over low heat for 5 minutes.

Add the cream and trout and let simmer over low heat for another 5 minutes, while turning.

Serve the trout, garnished with sauce. Accompany with white rice or pasta.

FILLET OF TROUT WITH MUSHROOMS

4 SERVINGS
Preparation Time: 15 minutes
Cooking Time: 20 minutes

2 tbsp	(25 ml) butter
1	green onion, sliced
1/2 tsp	(2 ml) minced garlic
1/2 cup	(125 ml) maple syrup
1 tsp	(5 ml) white vinegar
2 tbsp	(25 ml) Tamari or soy sauce
4	trout fillets, 6 oz (180 g) each
1 tbsp	(15 ml) butter
2	slices of bacon, chopped
1 1/2 cups	(375 ml) sliced mushrooms
2	green onions, sliced
2 tsp	(10 ml) all-purpose flour
1 cup	(250 ml) dry white wine or chicken stock, skimmed of fat
1/2 cup	(125 ml) 35% cream
	salt and pepper, to taste
2 tbsp	(25 ml) chopped, fresh parsley

Preheat the oven to 350°F (180°C). In a saucepan, melt the butter and lightly sauté the green onions. Add the garlic, maple syrup, vinegar and soy sauce. Bring to a boil and set aside.

Place the trout fillets in a greased, baking dish and cover with the maple sauce. Bake for 10 to 12 minutes. Keep warm.

In a frying pan, melt the butter and cook the bacon. Sprinkle in the flour and add the mushrooms and green onions and continue cooking for a few minutes. Add the white wine and cream and let simmer for 2 to 3 minutes; season and add the parsley.

Serve the trout fillets covered in mushroom sauce.

HALIBUT AND SCAMPI WITH BEER

4 SERVINGS

Preparation Time: 20 minutes

Cooking Time: 15 minutes

In a saucepan, melt the butter over low heat. Sauté the shallots, halibut, scallops and the scampi tails, being careful not to brown the butter. Season to taste.

Add the beer and stock; simmer over medium heat for 2 to 3 minutes. Remove the seafood and reduce the cooking stock by half.

1 tbsp	(15 ml) butter
2 tbsp	(25 ml) chopped shallots
1 lb	(500 g) halibut fillets, cut into pieces
8	scallops
12	scampi tails, shelled
	salt and white pepper, to taste
12 oz	(341 ml) beer
1 1/2 cups	(375 ml) fish or chicken stock, skimmed of fat
3/4 cup	(175 ml) 35% cream
1 tbsp	(15 ml) all purpose flour
1 tbsp	(15 ml) melted butter
GARNISH	
8	carrots
8	zucchini
8	potatoes
12	peapods
4	sprigs of dill

Add the cream and let simmer over medium heat for 2 to 3 minutes. Thicken the sauce with a mixture of flour and butter. Strain the sauce and return it to the saucepan. Put the seafood back into the pan and heat.

Serve on a platter with the vegetables. Garnish with a sprig of dill.

FILLET OF SOLE WITH FENNEL

4 SERVINGS

Preparation Time: 15 minutes

Cooking Time: 15 minutes

Preheat the oven to 400°F (200°C). Roll the sole fillets and place them in an baking dish with the fennel. Pour melted butter over top.

Bake the sole for approximately 10 minutes; season.

4	fillets of sole
1	small bulb of fennel approximately 1/2 lb (250 g), blanched and quartered
2 tbsp	(25 ml) melted butter
	salt and pepper, to taste
2 tbsp	(25 ml) fresh lemon juice
1/2 cup	(125 ml) dry white wine
3/4 cup	(175 ml) plain yogurt
GARNISH	
	fennel fronds

Add the lemon juice, white wine and yogurt. Continue baking for another 5 minutes.

When serving, garnish with fennel.

FILLET OF TROUT WITH COCONUT CREAM

4 SERVINGS
Preparation Time: 15 minutes
Cooking Time: 20 minutes

1 tsp	(5 ml) butter
2 tbsp	(25 ml) chopped shallots
1 tsp	(5 ml) curcuma
1 tsp	(5 ml) curry
1/2 tsp	(2 ml) cumin
2 tbsp	(25 ml) maple syrup
1/2 cup	(125 ml) dry white wine
1 cup	(250 ml) chicken stock, skimmed of fat
1 tsp	(5 ml) melted butter
1 tsp	(5 ml) flour
1/4 cup	(50 ml) 15% cream
	seasoning, to taste
1 tsp	(5 ml) vegetable oil
1 tsp	(5 ml) butter
4	trout fillets, skinned and deboned, cut in halfs

SEASONING
1/3 cup (75 ml) coconut cream

In a saucepan, melt the butter and lightly sauté the shallots. Sprinkle with curcuma, curry and cumin. Add the maple syrup then add the white wine and the chicken stock. Reduce by half and thicken with a mixture of butter and flour. Add the cream and let simmer for 1 to 2 minutes over low heat. Season and keep warm.

In a skillet, heat the oil and melt the butter. Cook the trout fillets for 2 to 3 minutes on each side, depending on their thickness, and season to taste.

When serving, add coconut cream to the sauce and pour over the trout fillets.

MIMOSA PASTRY WITH SALMON

4 SERVINGS

Preparation Time: 20 minutes
Cooking Time: 25 minutes

1 lb	(500 g) salmon fillets
8 oz	(250 g) flaky pastry dough
1 tbsp	(15 ml) butter
	salt and pepper, to taste
1 cup	(250 ml) rice, cooked and hot

GLAZE

1	egg
1 tbsp	(15 ml) milk

EGG SAUCE

1 tbsp	(15 ml) butter
1 tbsp	(15 ml) all-purpose flour
2 cups	(500 ml) warm milk
	salt and pepper, to taste
1 tbsp	(15 ml) white sauce thickener
3	hard boiled eggs, cut into pieces
1 tbsp	(15 ml) chopped, fresh parsley

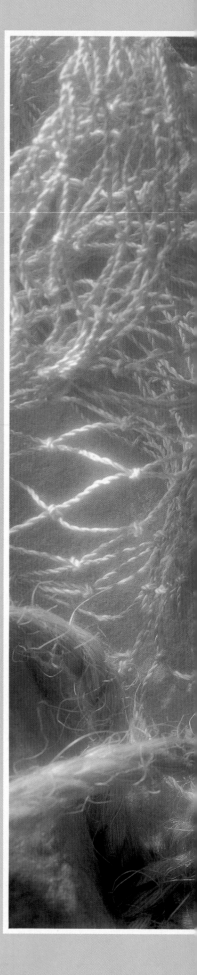

On a cutting board, cut the salmon fillets into eight scallops and keep refrigerated.

Preheat the oven to 350°F (180°C). On a flat surface, roll out the pastry dough and cut into four 4 in (10 cm) squares.

Place on a greased cookie sheet and brush with the egg and milk glaze. Bake for about 12 to 15 minutes or until the dough is golden.

EGG SAUCE

In a pan, melt the butter; add the flour and stir. Add warm milk, and simmer over low heat for 5 minutes; season. Thicken with the sauce thickener and add the eggs and parsley. Keep warm.

In a saucepan, melt the butter and cook the salmon scallops over low heat for 2 minutes on each side. Season to taste.

Cut the flaky pastry squares in half horizontally. Place the bottom half on a plate and garnish with rice and two salmon scallops. Add the egg sauce and cover with the other half of the flaky pastry.

BOSTON BLUE FISH WITH LENTILS

4 SERVINGS

Preparation Time: 15 minutes
Cooking Time: 1 hour

1/2 lb	(250 g) lentils
1 tbsp	(15 ml) butter
1/2 cup	(125 ml) chopped onions
1/2 cup	(125 ml) cubed celery
1 1/2 cups	(375 ml) carrot sticks
1 1/2 cups	(375 ml) turnip sticks
1 tsp	(5 ml) minced garlic
6 cups	(1.5L) chicken stock, skimmed of fat
1	bay leaf, stalk of thyme, and sprig of parsley salt and pepper, to taste
1 tbsp	(15 ml) corn oil
1 1/2 lb	(750 g) Boston blue fish fillets

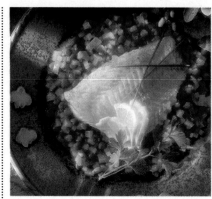

In a bowl, wash the lentils in lukewarm water. Set aside.

In a pan, heat the butter and sauté the onions, celery, carrots, turnip and garlic. Add the chicken stock, lentils, bay leaf, sprig of thyme and sprig of parsley. Season and let simmer over low heat for 45 minutes.

Preheat the oven to 400°F (200°C). In a pan, heat the oil and cook the Boston blue fish fillets over high heat, 1 minute on each side; season. Place the fillets on top of the lentils in a baking dish and bake in the oven for 15 minutes.

CALIFORNIA STYLE MAHI-MAHI

4 SERVINGS

Preparation Time: 15 minutes
Cooking Time: 25 minutes

2 cups	(500 ml) water
40	seedless green grapes
1 tbsp	(15 ml) butter
1 tbsp	(15 ml) chopped shallots
1 cup	(250 ml) dry white wine
4	Mahi-Mahi steaks, 16 oz (180 g) each (may substitute with halibut) salt and pepper, to taste
4	clusters of red grapes

BUTTER SAUCE

1/3 cup	(75 ml) chopped shallots
1 cup	(250 ml) dry white wine
1/2 lb	(250 g) cold butter cut into pieces salt and pepper, to taste

In a saucepan, boil the water and poach the grapes for 30 seconds. Drain and peel each individual grape. Using a food processor or an electric mixer, purée the grapes and set aside.

In a pan, melt the butter and add the shallots, white wine and Mahi Mahi; season. Cover and poach, for 10 to 12 minutes. Keep warm.

Add the grape purée and mix.

Put the Mahi-Mahi on a serving plate and cover with the sauce. Garnish with the whole red grapes.

BUTTER SAUCE

In a non-stick pan, combine the shallots and white wine. Simmer over medium heat until the mixture reduces by half. Strain the liquid and return to the pan. Add the shallot purée and warm over low heat. Add the pieces of butter, while stirring continuously.

Season and continue stirring until the sauce is thick and creamy.

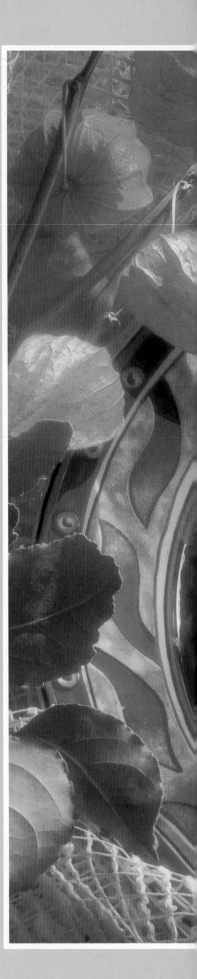

MACKEREL WITH MUSTARD AND SAUERKRAUT

4 SERVINGS
Preparation Time: 15 minutes
Cooking Time: 25 minutes

1/3 cup	(75 ml) butter
1 cup	(250 ml) sliced onion
2 cups	(500 ml) sauerkraut
3	bay leaves
12 oz	(341 ml) beer
1 cup	(250 ml) fish stock or chicken stock, skimmed of fat
1/2 cup	(125 ml) 35% cream
1 1/2 lb	(750 g) mackerel fillet
1 tbsp	(15 ml) Dijon mustard
	salt and pepper, to taste

In a saucepan, melt the butter and lightly sauté the onions.

Add the sauerkraut, and bay leaves, and lightly brown.

Add the beer and fish stock. Simmer over low heat for 5 minutes. Add the cream and continue cooking for 5 minutes.

Preheat the oven to 350°F (180°C). Place the sauerkraut on the bottom of a baking dish and place the mackerel fillets on top. Brush with Dijon mustard and season. Bake for 15 minutes.

THREE PEPPER SWORDFISH FROM NEIL'S HARBOR

8 SERVINGS
Preparation Time: 30 minutes
Cooking Time: 50 minutes

1	yellow pepper
1	red pepper
2	green peppers
1 oz	(30 g) spinach
8	6 oz (180 g) swordfish steaks, skinned and deboned
	salt and pepper, to taste

BUTTER SAUCE

1 tbsp	(15 ml) chopped shallots
1 tbsp	(15 ml) lemon juice
1 1/2 cups	(375 ml) white wine
1 1/2 cups	(375 ml) 15% cream
2 cups	(500 ml) softened butter

Boil the peppers in salted water for 20 minutes. Let cool and peel. Cut each pepper into pieces and seed. In a food processor, purée the peppers, one color at a time, and keep separate. Blanch the spinach and mix with the green peppers.

BUTTER SAUCE

In a saucepan, combine the shallots, lemon juice and wine. Cook over medium heat until reduced by a quarter. Add the cream and let reduce for 5 to 7 minutes. Cut the butter into cubes. Add to the mixture, one cube at a time, whipping after each addition until a smooth sauce is obtained.

Divide butter sauce into 3 portions and add to each pepper purée (do not mix colors). Place the sauce, individually, in a food processor and purée again. Keep warm.

Season the swordfish steaks to taste and cook on the barbecue (medium heat) for 7 to 10 minutes on each side. Keep warm.

Place the swordfish on the plates and garnish with the 3 pepper sauces.

GRILLED TURBOT WITH CITRUS FRUIT

4 SERVINGS
Preparation Time: 15 minutes
Cooking Time: 15 minutes

4	7 oz (200 g) fillets of turbot
4	sheets of aluminum foil
	sufficient quantity of butter
2	shallots, sliced
	pepper, to taste
1/2 cup	(125 ml) dry white wine
1	peeled lime, cut into wedges
1	peeled lemon, cut into wedges
1	peeled pink grapefruit, cut into wedges
2 tbsp	(25 ml) chopped, fresh parsley

Place each turbot fillet in the lightly buttered aluminum foil.

In a bowl, mix together all the other ingredients and spread the preparation on the fillets.

Place the fillets on the aluminum foil. Bring the edges of the foil over the fish and tightly crimp together to seal closed. Place on the barbecue grill, and cook for 12 to 15 minutes.

SEAFOOD BROCHETTES WITH BEER

4 SERVINGS

Preparation Time: 20 minutes
Cooking Time: 20 minutes

1/2 cup (125 ml) olive oil
12 oz (341 g) beer
2 tbsp (25 ml) lime juice
2 tbsp (25 ml) soya sauce
2 green onions, sliced
1 tsp (5 ml) minced garlic
2 tbsp (25 ml) chopped, fresh parsley
1 tbsp (15 ml) paprika
      chili peppers, to taste
      salt and pepper, to taste
8 jumbo shrimp, shelled and
      deveined
8 jumbo scallops
8 oz (250 g) salmon fillets,
      cut in pieces
8 round slices of carrot
8 pieces of green or red pepper
2 onions, quartered
4 cherry tomatoes
4 mushrooms

In a bowl, mix together the oil, beer, lime juice, soya sauce, green onion, garlic, parsley, paprika and chili peppers. Season to taste. Add the shrimp, scallops and salmon. Marinate for 1 to 2 hours in the refrigerator.

Soak wooden skewers in water, then thread the ingredients onto the skewers, alternating with the carrot slices. Finish with a cherry tomato, mushroom and pepper on each end. Grill on the barbecue for 8 to 10 minutes, turning regularly and brushing with the remaining marinade while cooking.

Serve with rice or couscous and a green salad.

GRILLED SALMON WITH TOMATO AND DILL SAUCE

4 SERVINGS

Preparation Time: 10 minutes
Cooking Time: 8 minutes

3/4 cup (175 ml) mayonnaise
1/2 cup (50 ml) chopped fresh
      dill or coriander
2 tbsp (25 ml) lime juice
1 tbsp (15 ml) milk
1/2 cup (125 ml) seedless diced tomatoes
4 salmon or halibut steaks
      approximately 1/2 in (2 cm) thick

In a bowl, mix together the mayonnaise, dill or coriander, lemon juice and milk. Place 1/2 cup (125 ml) of this mixture into a small bowl. Add the tomatoes, and let set.

Brush the salmon with the remaining mixture.

Grill on the barbecue for approximately 8 minutes, turning once. Serve with the dill and lime sauce.

FROM THE GRILL

GRILLED RED SNAPPER WITH FENNEL AND ALMONDS

4 SERVINGS

Preparation Time: 15 minutes
Cooking Time: 30 minutes

1/3 cup	(75 ml) vegetable oil
2 tbsp	(25 ml) lemon juice
2 tbsp	(25 ml) chopped fennel or fresh dill
1 tbsp	(15 ml) chopped, fresh parsley
1/4 cup	(50 ml) sliced almonds
	salt and pepper, to taste
1	red snapper, 3 to 4 lbs (1.5 to 2 kg)

In a bowl, mix together the oil, lemon juice, fennel, parsley and almonds; season.

Baste the red snapper (inside and out) with the marinade. Grill on a barbecue for 25 to 30 minutes, depending on the size.

Serve with lemon, butter and almonds.

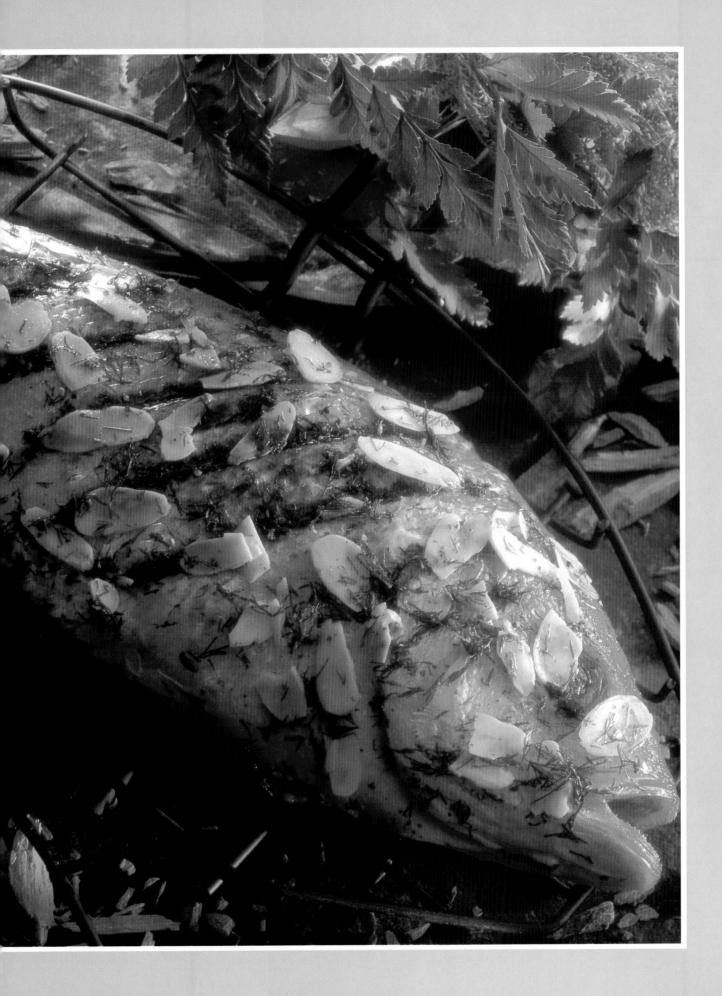

FILLET OF SEABASS

4 SERVINGS
Preparation Time: 15 minutes
Cooking Time: 15 minutes

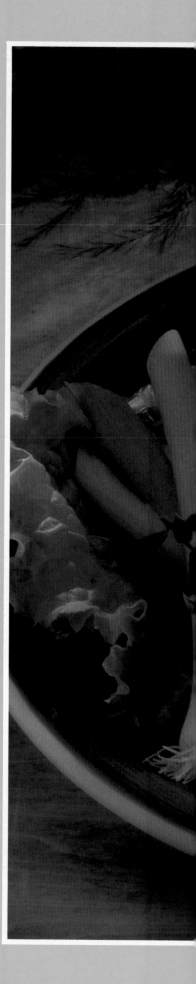

1/3 cup	(75 ml)	vegetable oil
2 tbsp	(25 ml)	lemon juice
1		medium sized egg
3		slices of bread, crumbled
1 tsp	(5 ml)	dry basil
1 cup	(250 ml)	diced tomatoes
1 tbsp	(15 ml)	chopped, fresh parsley
1		green onion, sliced
1 tsp	(5 ml)	minced garlic
		salt and pepper, to taste
4		seabass fillets, 6 oz/180 g
		vegetables of your choice
2		lemons, cut into wedges

In a bowl, mix together the oil, lemon juice, egg, bread, basil, tomatoes, parsley, green onions and garlic. Season and set aside.

Place two greased, 9 in (23 cm) aluminum foil squares on top of one another and place on a barbecue. Place the seabass and bread mixture onto the foil.

Grill for 12 to 15 minutes over high heat, with the barbecue lid down.

Transfer to plates and accompany with the vegetables of your choice. Garnish with lemon wedges.

NEW ENGLAND GRILLED LOBSTER

4 SERVINGS

Preparation Time: 10 minutes

Cooking Time: 30 minutes

4	1 1/2 lbs (750 g) live lobsters
1/2 cup	(125 ml) melted butter
1 tbsp	(15 ml) paprika
2 tbsp	(25 ml) Worcestershire sauce
1 cup	(250 ml) breadcrumbs
	salt and pepper, to taste

Cut each lobster in half, and set aside.

In a small bowl, mix together the butter, paprika, Worcestershire sauce, breadcrumbs, salt and pepper. Spread the mixture on the interior of the lobster.

Cook on an oiled grill, for 30 minutes, over low heat, with the cover closed. Serve.

WALL-EYED PIKE WITH RHUBARB

4 SERVINGS

Preparation Time: 10 minutes

Cooking Time: 15 minutes

4	sheets of aluminum foil
2 tbsp	(25 ml) butter
8	3 1/2 oz (100 g) pike fillets
1	green onion, sliced
2 cups	(500 ml) sliced, fresh or frozen rhubarb
	pepper, to taste
2 tbsp	(25 ml) chopped, fresh parsley

On each of the four sheets of aluminum foil, place a little butter and a pike fillet. Garnish with onions, rhubarb, pepper and parsley.

Securely fold the aluminum foil, covering the pike fillet, and grill on a barbecue for 15 minutes. Serve.

FROM THE GRILL

HADDOCK CAKES WITH FINE HERBS

4 SERVINGS

Preparation Time: 15 minutes
Cooking Time: 15 minutes

1 lb (500 g) haddock, chopped
1 medium sized egg
2 slices of bread, crumbled
1 green onion, coarsely sliced
1 tsp (5 ml) oregano
2 tbsp (25 ml) coarsely chopped, fresh parsley
1/2 cup (125 ml) wheat germ
salt and pepper, to taste
2 tbsp (25 ml) Italian breadcrumbs
2 tbsp (25 ml) grated Parmesan cheese

In a bowl or food processor, mix together the haddock, egg, bread, green onion, oregano, parsley and wheat germ; season.

Form into four balls and set aside.

Place two 9 in (23 cm) squares of aluminum foil onto the barbecue, one on top of the other.

Cook the balls on the aluminum foil for 5 to 6 minutes per side. Sprinkle with breadcrumbs and Parmesan cheese. Cover and cook for another 2 to 3 minutes.

Serve with mixed vegetables.

FRESH SALMON WITH JUMBO SHRIMP

4 SERVINGS

Preparation Time: 15 minutes
Cooking Time: 17 minutes

1/2 cup (125 ml) dry white wine
2 tbsp (25 ml) chopped, fresh coriander
2 tbsp (25 ml) lemon juice
1 tbsp (15 ml) corn oil
4 fresh salmon fillets, 4 oz (120 g) each
4 sheets of aluminum foil
salt and pepper, to taste
12 jumbo shrimp, deveined and peeled

In a bowl, mix together the white wine, coriander, lemon juice and oil.

Place the salmon on the aluminum foil and cover with the wine base mixture; season. Bring up the edges of the foil and tightly crimp together to seal closed. Cook on a grill over medium heat for 12 minutes.

Thread the shrimp onto mini skewers and return to the grill for 5 minutes.

Place salmon and shrimp on plates.

FROM THE GRILL

LOBSTER RAVIOLI

4 TO 6 SERVINGS

Preparation Time: 20 minutes
Cooking Time: 25 minutes

WON TON

2	cooked lobsters
1	medium egg
1	green onion, sliced
2 tbsp	(25 ml) chopped, fresh parsley
1 tsp	(5 ml) curcuma
	salt and pepper, to taste
1	box of won ton dough
1 cup	(250 ml) fish stock or
	chicken stock, skimmed of fat
2 cups	(500 ml) water

SAUCE

2 tbsp	(25 ml) olive oil
1 cup	(250 ml) sliced onions
1/2 cup	(125 ml) sliced celery
1/2 cup	(125 ml) sliced carrots
1	bay leaf, 1 stalk of thyme,
	1 sprig of parsley
	salt and pepper, to taste
1 tsp	(5 ml) curry
1/2 tsp	(2 ml) cumin
2 tbsp	(25 ml) curcuma
1/4 tsp	(1 ml) nutmeg
1 tsp	(5 ml) carvi seeds
1 cup	(250 ml) rice wine or
	dry white wine
3 cups	(750 ml) fish stock or
	chicken stock, skimmed of fat
1 tbsp	(15 ml) butter
1 tbsp	(15 ml) all-purpose flour
1/2 cup	(125 ml) 35% cream

GARNISH

4 to 6	cherry tomatoes
8 to 12	chives

WON TON

On a flat surface, separate the lobster meat from the shell. Keep the shell and set it aside. Cut the meat into small pieces and place it in a bowl. Incorporate the egg, green onions, parsley and curcuma; season.

Stuff the won ton dough with the mixture and close. Secure the sides with water. In a casserole, bring the fish stock and water to a boil and poach the ravioli for 1 to 2 minutes over low heat. Cool and set aside.

SAUCE

In a saucepan, heat the oil and brown the lobster shells (cut into pieces), onions, celery, carrots, bay leaf, thyme and parsley. Season to taste. Add the curry, cumin, curcuma, nutmeg, carvi seeds, rice wine and stock. Let simmer for 15 to 20 minutes over low heat. Strain and return to the stove. Add the mixture of butter and flour. Add the cream and let simmer for 2 to 3 minutes.

Serve the ravioli covered in sauce. Garnish with cherry tomatoes and chives.

SHRIMP BROCHETTES

4 SERVINGS

Preparation Time: 25 minutes
Cooking Time: 10-15 minutes

12	cherry tomatoes
24	jumbo shrimp, peeled and deveined
8	round slices of zucchini
8	baby corns
1	green pepper, cut into eight pieces
	salt and pepper, to taste

MARJORAM SAUCE

2 tbsp	(25 ml) butter
2 tbsp	(25 ml) chopped shallots
1/2 cup	(125 ml) dry white wine
1 cup	(250 ml) vegetable juice
1/4 cup	(50 ml) brown sauce thickener
1	tomato, peeled, seeded and diced
2 tbsp	(25 ml) chopped, fresh marjoram
	or 2 tsp (10 ml) dry marjoram
2 tbsp	(25 ml) chopped, fresh parsley

MARJORAM SAUCE

In a saucepan, melt the butter; add the shallots and lightly brown. Add the white wine. Add the vegetable juice and reduce by one third. Thicken with the sauce thickener. Add the tomatoes, marjoram and parsley. Set aside.

Preheat the oven to 400°F (200°C). Alternating, thread the ingredients onto the skewers, beginning with the cherry tomatoes, and season to taste.

Place the brochettes on a cookie sheet, baste with marjoram sauce and bake for 8 to 10 minutes.

Serve the brochettes with the remaining sauce.

MEDLEY OF MUSSELS AND SHRIMP

4 SERVINGS

Preparation Time: 15 minutes

Cooking Time: 10 minutes

2 tbsp	(25 ml) olive oil
2 tbsp	(25 ml) chopped shallots
1 tsp	(5 ml) minced garlic
16	shrimp, peeled and deveined
12 oz	(341 ml) beer
28 oz	(796 ml) crushed and peeled tomatoes with fine herbs
32	mussels, cleaned and debearded
2 tbsp	(25 ml) chopped, fresh parsley
	salt and pepper, to taste
1 tbsp	(15 ml) cornstarch, diluted in a bit of water
1/2 cup	(125 ml) chopped, fresh basil (optional)

In a large saucepan, heat the oil and sauté the shallots. Add the garlic, shrimp, beer and tomatoes. Bring to a boil and remove the shrimp.

Add the mussels and parsley; season. Cover and let simmer for 5 minutes or until the mussels are opened. Thicken the sauce with the cornstarch. Return the shrimp to the pan and add the basil. Mix well and serve.

Discard any mussels that have not opened after cooking.

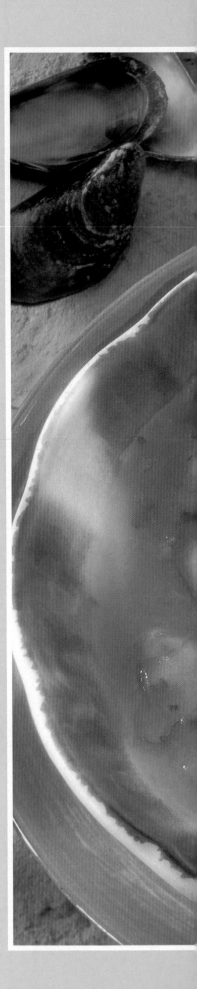

SHRIMP & RICOTTA SOUFFLE

4 SERVINGS

Preparation Time: 15 minutes

Cooking Time: 30 minutes

1 tbsp	(15 ml) butter
1	green onion, chopped
1 tbsp	(15 ml) all-purpose flour
1/2 cup	(125 ml) 15% cream
1/2 cup	(125 ml) ricotta cheese
1/2 cup	(125 ml) milk
	salt and pepper, to taste
1/2 cup	(125 ml) chopped Nordic shrimp
3	medium egg whites, whisked to form soft peaks

Preheat the oven to 380°F (180°C). In a saucepan, melt the butter; add the green onions and cook for 1 minute over very low heat. Be careful not to brown the butter.

Add the flour and cream. Let simmer for 5 minutes over low heat. Incorporate the cheese and milk and continue cooking for 5 minutes; season. Add the shrimp and pour into a bowl. Refrigerate for 15 to 20 minutes.

Gently fold in the egg whites with a spatula or wooden spoon.

Pour the mixture into 4 small, greased soufflé molds. Bake for about 20 minutes and serve immediately.

TOMATO AND SHRIMP QUICHE

4 SERVINGS

Preparation Time: 15 minutes
Cooking Time: 50 minutes

12	slices of bread
6	medium eggs
2 cups	(500 ml) milk
1 tbsp	(15 ml) cornstarch
	salt and pepper, to taste
2	medium tomatoes, sliced
2	green onions, sliced
1/4 cup	(50 ml) chopped, fresh basil or 1 tsp (5 ml) dried basil
1 cup	(250 ml) grated cheddar cheese
1 cup	(250 ml) Nordic shrimp

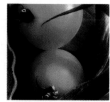

Preheat the oven to 350°F (180°C). On a flat surface, flatten the slices of bread using a rolling pin. In four greased aluminum pans of average size (or quiche dishes), place 3 slices of bread to cover the bottom and the sides. Bake for 12 to 15 minutes until golden. Set aside.

In a bowl, mix together the eggs, cornstarch and milk; season and set aside.

Garnish the slices of bread with tomatoes, green onions, basil, cheese and shrimp. Cover with the egg mixture and bake for 30 to 35 minutes.

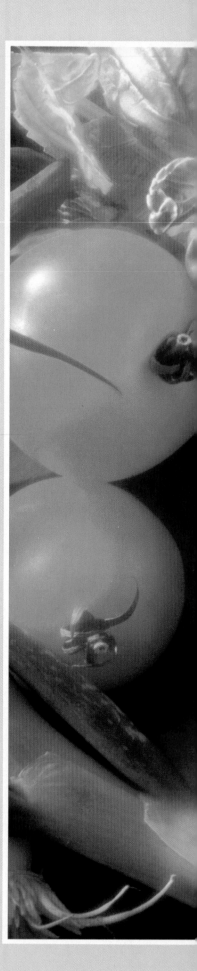

SIERRA MADRE SHRIMP

4 SERVINGS

Preparation Time: 10 minutes
Cooking Time: 6 minutes

1/4 cup	(50 ml) olive oil
1/2 cup	(125 ml) dry white wine
1/4 cup	(50 ml) lime juice
1/4 cup	(50 ml) chopped, fresh coriander or parsley
1	dash of ground Jamaican pepper
	pepper, to taste
1 1/2 lb	(750 g) jumbo shrimp, peeled and deveined

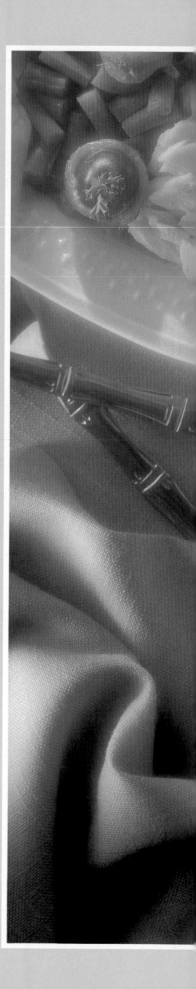

In a bowl, mix together the olive oil, white wine, lime juice, coriander, Jamaican pepper and ground pepper.

Place the shrimp in a glass dish and pour the marinade on top. Cover and let marinate for a minimum of 3 hours or overnight.

Preheat the oven. Soak eight wooden skewers in cold water for 15 minutes and thread the shrimp onto the skewers. Place the brochettes on a greased baking sheet and broil in the oven for 3 minutes on each side. Baste with the marinade. Serve with rice pilaf.

ALASKAN SCALLOPS WITH WILD MUSHROOMS

4 SERVINGS

Preparation Time: 15 minutes

Cooking Time: 20 minutes

2 tbsp	(25 ml) butter
20	scallops
1/2 lb	(250 g) girolle mushrooms or oyster mushrooms
2 tbsp	(25 ml) chopped shallots
	salt and pepper, to taste
1 cup	(250 ml) dry white wine
1 cup	(250 ml) 35% cream
1 tbsp	(15 ml) butter
1 tbsp	(15 ml) flour
GARNISH	
	chives

In a saucepan, melt the butter over low heat and lightly sauté the scallops, shallots and mushrooms for approximately 2 minutes. Season to taste.

Add white wine and let simmer for 2 minutes. Remove the scallops and mushrooms. Keep warm. Add the cream and reduce by one third.

Thicken with a mixture of butter and flour, let simmer a few minutes. Strain the sauce.

Line the serving plates with sauce, place the scallops on the plate and garnish with mushrooms and chives.

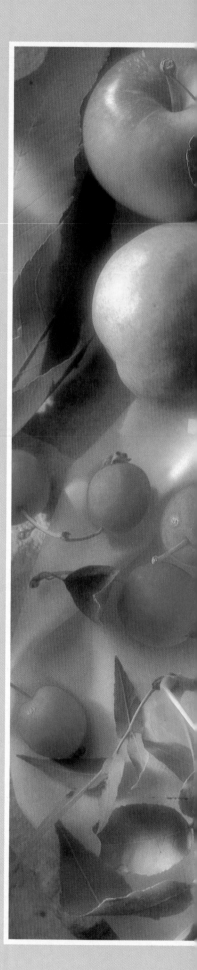

SAUTÉED LOBSTER, NOVA SCOTIA STYLE

4 SERVINGS
Preparation Time: 30 minutes
Cooking Time: 5 to 8 minutes

11.3 oz	(320 g) frozen lobster or 2 cups (500 ml) fresh lobster, in pieces
1 lb	(500 g) spinach fettuccini, cooked and hot
2 tbsp	(25 ml) olive oil
1/2 cup	(125 ml) lobster juice
1/4 cup	(50 ml) 35% cream
1/4 cup	(50 ml) olive oil
1 1/2 tsp	(7 ml) cornstarch
1 tsp	(5 ml) mustard seed
1	garlic clove, minced
1	red pepper, chopped
8	large mushrooms, sliced
	juice of 1/2 lemon
1/2 tsp	(2 ml) salt (optional)
1/4 cup	(50 ml) chopped, fresh parsley

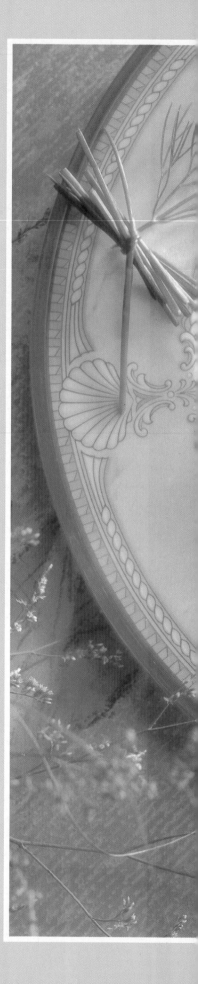

Thaw the lobster and drain. Reserve the juice. Cut the lobster into pieces, and set aside. Reserve the claws for garnish. Add the olive oil to the pasta and keep warm.

In a bowl, combine the lobster juice and cream. Add the cornstarch and stir until smooth. Set aside.

Heat the oil in a wok or in a large covered pan. Add the mustard seed and cover immediately (the seeds will pop vigorously). Shake the pan for 20 to 30 seconds or until all the seeds have stopped popping. Reduce the heat and add the garlic, red peppers, mushrooms, lemon juice and salt. Cook for 2 minutes.

Add the lobster, parsley and lobster juice mixture. Cook until the lobster is very hot. Place the fettuccini on the plates and pour the sauce over top. Garnish with lobster claws and fresh parsley.

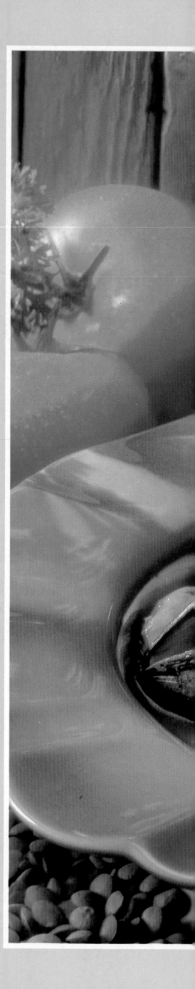

MUSSEL AND LENTIL STEW

4 SERVINGS

Preparation Time: 20 minutes

Cooking Time: 1 hour

1 tbsp	(15 ml)	butter
2 tbsp	(25 ml)	chopped shallots
2 lb	(1 kg)	mussels, cleaned and debearded
1 tbsp	(15 ml)	chopped, fresh parsley
1 tsp	(5 ml)	minced garlic
28 g	(796 ml)	tomatoes with fine herbs, peeled
2 cups	(500 ml)	beer
		salt and pepper, to taste
1 1/2 cups	(375 ml)	lentils
1/2 cup	(175 ml)	sliced carrots
1/2 cup	(175 ml)	sliced celery
1 cup	(250 ml)	sliced mushrooms

 In a large pan, melt the butter and lightly sauté the shallots. Add the mussels, parsley, garlic, tomatoes and beer, season to taste. Bring to a boil. Cover and simmer for 5 minutes, or until mussels are completely opened. Remove the mussels from their shells. Keep a few full mussels for decoration.

Add the lentils, carrots, celery and mushrooms to the cooking stock. Bring to a boil, cover and let simmer over light heat for about 45 minutes. Add the mussels and sprinkle with parsley. If necessary, thicken with a bit of cornstarch.

SCALLOPS WITH OLIVE OIL

4 SERVINGS

Preparation Time: 20 minutes
Cooking Time: 25 minutes

RICE

2 tbsp	(25 ml) olive oil
1 1/2 cups	(375 ml) long grain rice
1	pinch of salt
2	bay leaves
4 cups	(1 L) water

SCALLOPS

28	jumbo scallops (or 72 medium)
	salt and pepper, to taste
2 tbsp	(25 ml) all-purpose flour
1/4 cup	(50 ml) olive oil
2 tbsp	(25 ml) chopped, fresh parsley
2 tbsp	(25 ml) lemon juice

SALAD

1/4 cup	(50 ml) olive oil
	salt and pepper, to taste
1 tsp	(5 ml) minced garlic
2 tbsp	(25 ml) lemon juice
8 cups	(2 L) Romaine lettuce

RICE

In a saucepan, heat the oil and brown the rice. Add the salt, 2 bay leaves and water and bring to a boil. Continue cooking over low heat until the water has completely evaporated. Turn off the heat and keep covered until ready to serve.

SCALLOPS

Wash and dry the scallops on a paper towel. Place in a bowl, then add salt, pepper and flour. In a large pan, heat the olive oil and brown the scallops for 1 to 2 minutes on each side. Lower the heat and add the parsley and lemon juice; set aside.

SALAD

In a large bowl, mix together the olive oil, salt, pepper and garlic. Add the lettuce and toss. Serve the scallops with rice and salad. Garnish with vegetables.

JAZZY SHRIMP CASSEROLE

4 SERVINGS

Preparation Time: 10 minutes
Cooking Time: 13 minutes

2 tbsp	(25 ml) butter
2	onions, chopped
1	celery stalk, chopped
3	garlic cloves, minced
1 tsp	(5 ml) thinly sliced jalapeno peppers
2 tbsp	(25 ml) potato starch
14 oz	(398 ml) Italian tomatoes
1 tbsp	(15 ml) paprika
	salt and pepper, to taste
1	pinch Cayenne pepper
2 lb	(1 kg) shrimp
4	green onions, thinly sliced
1/2 cup	(125 ml) finely chopped, fresh parsley

In a saucepan, melt the butter over medium heat and sauté the onions, celery, garlic and jalapeno peppers for 5 minutes. Add the potato starch and mix well.

Add the tomatoes, paprika, salt, pepper and Cayenne pepper. Let simmer for 5 minutes.

Add the shrimp and cook for 3 minutes. Add the green onions and parsley. Serve on a bed of steamed white rice.